Ladybugs

Ladybugs

M. C. McBee

THE CHILD'S WORLD®

The Child's World

Published in the United States of America by The Child's World®
PO Box 326
Chanhassen, MN 55317-0326
800-599-READ
www.childsworld.com

Project Manager Mary Berendes
Editor Katherine Stevenson, Ph.D.
Designer Mary Berendes
**Our sincere thanks to Robert Mitchell, Ph.D.,
for his input and guidance on this book.**

Photo Credits
© Andrew Syred/SPL/Photo Researchers Inc.: 30
ANIMALS ANIMALS © Bates Littlehales: 19
ANIMALS ANIMALS © E. R. Degginger: 24
ANIMALS ANIMALS © James H. Robinson: 16
ANIMALS ANIMALS © Stephen Dalton: 10 (bottom)
© Bill Johnson: 23
© Bob Marsh; Papilio/CORBIS: 15 (main)
© Dwight Kuhn: 10 (top)
© Gary Braasch/CORBIS: 26
© Hugh Clark; Frank Lane Picture Agency/CORBIS: 9
© Ken Wilson; Papilio/CORBIS: 15 (inset)
© Naturfoto Honal/CORBIS: 29
© Philip James Corwin/CORBIS: 6
© Robert Pickett/CORBIS: 13
© Robert & Linda Mitchell: 20
© 2003 Salt & Light Productions/Raw Talent Photo: cover
© Taxi/Steve Hopkin: 2

Library of Congress Cataloging-in-Publication Data
McBee, M. C., 1973–
Ladybugs / by M. C. McBee.
p. cm.
ISBN 1-56766-979-4 (lib. bdg. : alk. paper)
1. Ladybugs—Juvenile literature. [1. Ladybugs.] I. Title.
QL596.C65 M33 2003
595.76'9—dc21
2001000503

On the cover...

Front cover: This ladybug is resting on a leaf.
Page 2: This seven-spotted ladybug is walking on a flower in England.

Table of Contents

You are lying in a field of grass on a warm summer day. You watch clouds of different shapes roll by. A breeze picks up, and the green grass waves and bends. Suddenly, you feel a little tickle on your hand. A small red and black creature is crawling slowly along your skin. What is this tiny animal? It's a ladybug!

⇐ This ladybug is slowly walking on a girl's hand.

What Are Ladybugs?

Ladybugs have many other names, including "lady beetles" or "ladybird beetles." Ladybugs are a kind of **insect**. All insects have a body that is divided into three areas. The front area is the head. The middle area is the **thorax**, or chest. The back area is the **abdomen**, or stomach region. Insects also have six legs and one or two pairs of wings.

This seven-spotted ladybug is walking on a blade of grass. ⇒

Ladybugs are beetles. Like other beetles, ladybugs have two pairs of wings—a hard outer pair and a soft inner pair. The hard, shell-like outer wings aren't used for flying. Instead, they protect the soft inner wings underneath. The inner wings are the only ones used for flying. When a ladybug is ready to fly, it opens its outer wings and spreads its inner wings. When it lands, it closes its outer wings and tucks its soft wings underneath them.

⇐ *Top*: Here you can see this ladybug's soft inner wings.

Bottom: This ladybug is just taking off from a flower.

Are There Different Kinds of Ladybugs?

There are about 4,500 different kinds, or **species**, of ladybugs. They live all over the world, from the United States to Mexico to Australia. They usually live in wooded areas and grassy fields.

All ladybug species have rounded bodies. They range in size from about 3 millimeters (this big ●) to around 10 millimeters (this big ⬤). Most ladybug species have black and white markings with red outer wings. Others have yellow and white outer wings. Some ladybugs are completely black.

Seven-spotted ladybugs like this one are very common. ⇒

Most ladybugs are named after their markings. *Two-spotted ladybugs* have two large spots. *Parenthesis ladybugs* have spots that look like parentheses. *Three-banded ladybugs* have three black stripes on their orange wings. *Eye-spotted ladybugs* have yellow-ringed spots that look like eyes.

Other ladybugs have different names. The *twice-stabbed ladybug* is black with two reddish spots. *Polished ladybugs* are pinkish red with no spots. *Crypts* have a tan head and black outer wings. Their "crypts" nickname is short for their scientific name, which is hard to spell and pronounce (*Cryptolaemus montrouzieri*).

Main photo: Why do you think twice-stabbed ⇒ ladybugs like this one got their name?

Small photo: This 22-spotted ladybug is creeping over a leaf.

Ladybugs fly from place to place looking for food. They are always hungry and are constantly searching for their next meal. Some ladybugs eat plants and leaves. Most, however, eat other insects. Mites and plant lice are tasty treats for ladybugs, but aphids (AY-fids) are their favorite meal.

Aphids are tiny insects that drink the juices of plants. In large numbers, aphids can be a big problem because they destroy the plants they eat. But not when ladybugs are around! Ladybugs can eat lots of aphids in a short time. In fact, some farmers use ladybugs to help keep aphids under control.

⇐ This Asian ladybug is eating aphids.

What Happens to Ladybugs in the Winter?

Like most insects, ladybugs can't survive freezing temperatures. When the weather turns colder, most ladybugs head for a warm place to rest for the winter. This long rest is called **hibernation**. Spaces under rocks, porches, and old logs are favorite hibernation spots. There the ladybugs are protected from the harsh cold and wind. Ladybugs don't usually hibernate by themselves—in fact, several hundred often share the same spot.

This tree in South Dakota is covered with ⇒ ladybugs gathering in the cool fall weather.

When the warm spring weather arrives, the ladybugs wake up. They start to fly everywhere, feeding and looking for mates. After a male and female mate, the female looks for safe places to lay her eggs. Usually she lays them on the undersides of leaves. The female lays about 50 yellow eggs in each spot. She might lay up to 200 eggs before she is done. About 8 days later, the baby ladybugs (called **larvae**) hatch. The hungry larvae start searching for food right away.

⇐ These eggs were laid by a twice-stabbed ladybug.

Ladybug larvae don't look anything like their parents. Instead of being smooth and round, the larvae are long and spiny. They have large jaws, called **mandibles**, that they use to capture and eat other insects. The larvae grow quickly. As they grow, they shed their hard outer skin, or **exoskeleton**, three times.

After about three weeks, the larvae stop eating. They find a safe resting place on a leaf or a branch. Soon each larva's exoskeleton splits open, revealing a new body shape. The larvae are now called **pupae**. The pupae remain very still for the next few days. Their bodies undergo many changes as they form into adults. After about a week, their exoskeletons break open, and the new adults come out. This process of going from egg to adult is called **metamorphosis**.

Top: Ladybug larvae like this one don't look anything like adults. ⇒

Bottom: This ladybug pupa is beginning to look more like an adult.

Most ladybugs eat insect pests that damage flowers and crops. Many farmers and gardeners like to have ladybugs around. Then they don't have to use as many harmful chemicals to protect their crops. Sometimes farmers release thousands of ladybugs into orchards and fields.

But not all ladybugs are helpful. Instead of eating other insects, some ladybugs eat plants. The *Mexican bean beetle* loves to nibble on bean plants. The *squash beetle* eats squashes and pumpkins. Both of these ladybugs can damage crops if they are not controlled.

⇐ Here you can see an adult Mexican bean beetle as well as some larvae and pupae. They are damaging the leaf they are feeding on.

Ladybugs do not have many natural enemies. Spiders eat unlucky ladybugs that stumble into their webs. Large praying mantids also eat ladybugs if given the chance. But the biggest threat to ladybugs is people. By using bug sprays and other chemicals on their gardens or crops, people often kill helpful ladybugs by mistake.

⇐ This orb weaver spider has caught a ladybug to eat.

How Do Ladybugs Stay Safe?

Even though they have few enemies, ladybugs are still able to protect themselves if they sense danger. Scientists think that ladybugs taste bad to birds and other insect-eating animals. Ladybugs also give off a bad smell that many other animals dislike. If a ladybug senses danger, it often plays dead by dropping to the ground and holding very still. When the danger is gone, the ladybug simply gets up and goes about its business.

Here you can see a red wood ant attacking a ladybug. ⇒

People have been fascinated by ladybugs for a very long time. Many stories and legends have been written about them. Long ago, people thought that seeing ladybugs meant good weather was coming. Some thought that seeing ladybugs meant a good growing season for crops. Others thought that a young lady who saw a ladybug crawling on her hand would marry soon. Ladybugs were often considered lucky—especially the ones with seven spots.

The next time a little ladybug tickles your arm, try watching it for a while. See if you can count its spots and guess what species it belongs to. And then think about your good luck—you've been touched by a lucky ladybug!

⇐ This picture shows a seven-spotted ladybug as it takes off from a flower. The picture was taken with a special magnifying tool called a SEM.

Glossary

abdomen (AB-doh-men)
The back area of an insect is its abdomen, or stomach region. Ladybugs have an abdomen.

exoskeleton (eks-oh-SKEL-eh-tun)
An exoskeleton is a hard outer covering some animals have instead of bones. Ladybug larvae shed their exoskeletons several times as they grow.

hibernation (hy-bur-NAY-shun)
Hibernation is a long rest some animals take in the winter, slowing down their bodies until spring comes. Ladybugs hibernate under rocks and logs.

insect (IN-sekt)
Insects are animals that have six legs, one or two pairs of wings, and a body that is divided into three areas. Ladybugs are insects.

larvae (LAR-vee)
Larvae are young insects between the egg stage and the pupa stage of life. Ladybug larvae are long and spiny.

mandibles (MAN-dih-bullz)
Mandibles are jaws that many animals have for biting their food. Ladybug larvae have mandibles.

metamorphosis (meh-tuh-MOR-fuh-siss)
Metamorphosis is the series of changes some animals go through while growing from egg to adult. Ladybugs go through metamorphosis.

pupae (PYOO-pee)
Pupae are young insects that are not quite adults. Ladybug pupae stay very still while their bodies change into their adult shapes.

species (SPEE-sheez)
A species is a different type of an animal. There are about 4,500 different species of ladybugs.

thorax (THOR-ax)
The thorax is the chest area of an insect. Ladybugs have a thorax.

Index

Web Sites

Visit our homepage for lots of links about ladybugs!

http://www.childsworld.com/links.html

Note to Parents, Teachers, and Librarians:
We routinely verify our Web links to make sure they're safe, active sites— so encourage your readers to check them out!